20 best cake pops recipes

Houghton Mifflin Harcourt
Boston • New York • 2013

Copyright © 2013 by General Mills, Minneapolis, Minnesota. All rights reserved.

For information about permission to reproduce selections from this book, write to Permissions, Houghton Mifflin Harcourt Publishing Company, 215 Park Avenue South, New York, New York 10003.

www.hmhco.com

Cover photo: Sports Ball Cake Pops (page 10)

General Mills
Food Content and Relationship Marketing Director: Geoff Johnson
Food Content Marketing Manager: Susan Klobuchar
Senior Editor: Grace Wells
Kitchen Manager: Ann Stuart
Recipe Development and Testing: Betty Crocker Kitchens
Photography: General Mills Photography Studios and Image Library

Houghton Mifflin Harcourt
Publisher: Natalie Chapman
Editorial Director: Cindy Kitchel
Executive Editor: Anne Ficklen
Associate Editor: Heather Dabah
Managing Editor: Rebecca Springer
Production Editor: Kristi Hart
Cover Design: Chrissy Kurpeski
Book Design: Tai Blanche

ISBN 978-0-544-31471-9
Printed in the United States of America

The Betty Crocker Kitchens seal guarantees success in your kitchen. Every recipe has been tested in America's Most Trusted Kitchens™ to meet our high standards of reliability, easy preparation and great taste.

FIND MORE GREAT IDEAS AT
BettyCrocker.com

Dear Friends,

This new collection of colorful mini books has been put together with you in mind because we know that you love great recipes and enjoy cooking and baking but have a busy lifestyle. So every little book in the series contains just 20 recipes for you to treasure and enjoy. Plus, each book is a single subject designed in a bite-size format just for you—it's easy to use and is filled with favorite recipes from the Betty Crocker Kitchens!

All of the books are conveniently divided into short chapters so you can quickly find what you're looking for, and the beautiful photos throughout are sure to entice you into making the delicious recipes. In the series, you'll discover a fabulous array of recipes to spark your interest—from cookies, cupcakes and birthday cakes to party ideas for a variety of occasions. There's grilled foods, potluck favorites and even gluten-free recipes too.

You'll love the variety in these mini books—so pick one or choose them all for your cooking pleasure.

Enjoy and happy cooking!

Sincerely,

Betty Crocker

contents

Kids' Parties
Brownie Pops · 6
Cheerios®-Banana Cake Pops · 7
Trix® Cereal Cake Pops · 8
Gusher® Confetti Cake Balls · 9
Sports Ball Cake Pops · 10
Watermelon Cake Pops · 11
Cookies-and-Cream Cake Pops · 12
Scaredy Cat Cake Pops · 13
Witchy Cake Balls · 14

Special Occasions
Strawberries-and-Cream Cake Pops · 15
Lemon Meringue Cake Pops · 16
Tequila Sunrise Cake Pops · 17
Chocolate-Covered Cherry Cake Pops · 18
Boston Cream Cake Pops · 19
Raspberry-Chocolate Cake Pops · 20
Cappuccino Cake Pops · 22
Maple-Walnut Cake Pops · 23
Bourbon-Spiked Brownie Truffle Balls · 24
Cake Ball Ornaments · 25
Holiday Cake Bon Bons · 26

Metric Conversion Guide · 28
Recipe Testing and Calculating
    Nutrition Information · 29

Kids' Parties

Brownie Pops
Prep Time: 30 Minutes • **Start to Finish:** 2 Hours 45 Minutes • Makes 15 brownie pops

1 box (1 lb 2.4 oz) Betty Crocker Original Supreme Premium brownie mix

Water, vegetable oil and egg called for on brownie mix box

15 paper lollipop sticks

1 package (14 oz) red candy melts or coating wafers

Red decorating sugar or candy sprinkles

1 block of white plastic craft foam

1 Heat oven to 350°F (325°F for dark or nonstick pan). Grease 8- or 9-inch square pan with shortening or cooking spray.

2 Make brownies as directed on box, using water, oil and egg. Bake as directed on box. Cool completely, about 1 hour.

3 Place pan of brownies in freezer 30 minutes. Cut brownies into 15 rectangular bars, 5 rows by 3 rows. Roll each rectangle into a ball.

4 In small microwavable bowl, microwave candy melts uncovered on Medium (50%) 1 minute; stir. Continue microwaving and stirring in 5-second increments until melted; stir until smooth. Dip tip of 1 lollipop stick about ½ inch into melted candy and carefully insert stick into 1 brownie ball no more than halfway. Dip brownie ball into melted candy to cover; tap off excess. (Reheat candy in microwave or add vegetable oil if too thick to coat.) Immediately sprinkle with decorating sugar. Poke opposite end of stick into foam block.

1 Brownie Pop: Calories 360; Total Fat 15g (Saturated Fat 8g, Trans Fat 0g); Cholesterol 30mg; Sodium 180mg; Total Carbohydrate 55g (Dietary Fiber 0g); Protein 2g **Carbohydrate Choices:** 3½

Cheerios-Banana Cake Pops

Prep Time: 3 Hours 25 Minutes • **Start to Finish:** 7 Hours • Makes 60 cake pops

- 1 box Betty Crocker SuperMoist® yellow cake mix
- 1 cup mashed very ripe bananas (2 medium)
- ½ cup vegetable oil
- ¼ cup water
- 3 eggs
- 2½ bags (14 oz each) yellow candy melts
- 60 paper lollipop sticks
- 3½ cup Chocolate Cheerios cereal
- 3½ cup Peanut Butter Cheerios cereal
- 1 block of white plastic craft foam

1 Heat oven to 325°F (325°F for dark or nonstick pan). Spray nonstick cake pop baking pan with baking spray with flour.

2 In large bowl, beat cake mix, bananas, oil, water and eggs with electric mixer on low speed 30 seconds. Beat on medium speed 2 minutes, scraping bowl occasionally until smooth. In bottom half of pan (without holes), fill each well with 1 level measuring tablespoon of cake batter. Place top half of pan on top and secure with keys. (Cover remaining cake batter with plastic wrap; place in refrigerator.) Bake 18 to 22 minutes or until toothpick inserted in center comes out clean. Cool 5 minutes. Remove cake balls from pan; cool completely on cooling rack. Repeat with remaining cake batter, cleaning and spraying pan before filling with batter.

3 In microwavable bowl, microwave 1 bag of candy melts uncovered on Medium (50%) 1 minute, then in 15-second increments, until melted; stir until smooth. Before dipping cake balls, trim edges of baked cake balls. Dip tip of 1 lollipop stick about ½ inch into melted candy and carefully insert stick into 1 cake ball no more than halfway. Dip cake ball into melted candy to cover; tap off excess. (Reheat candy in microwave or add vegetable oil if too thick to coat.) Immediately place cereal onto coated cake pops to decorate. Poke opposite end of stick into foam block. Repeat with remaining cake pops and candy melts.

1 Cake Pop: Calories 150; Total Fat 7g (Saturated Fat 5g, Trans Fat 0g); Cholesterol 10mg; Sodium 100mg; Total Carbohydrate 22g (Dietary Fiber 0g); Protein 0gnc **Carbohydrate Choices:** 1½

Tip For a fun display, place the foam block in a cereal bowl. Insert the cake pops into the foam block. Cover the foam block with extra Cheerios cereal.

Trix Cereal Cake Pops

Prep Time: 1 Hour 15 Minutes • **Start to Finish:** 5 Hours 45 Minutes • Makes 48 cake pops

- 1 box Betty Crocker SuperMoist yellow or white cake mix
- Water, vegetable oil and eggs or egg whites called for on cake mix box
- 1 container (1 lb) Betty Crocker Rich & Creamy vanilla frosting
- 4 cups Trix cereal
- 36 oz vanilla-flavored candy coating (almond bark)
- 48 paper lollipop sticks
- 1 block of white plastic craft foam

1 Heat oven to 350°F (325°F for dark or nonstick pan). Make and bake cake as directed on box for 13 x 9-inch pan. Cool completely, about 1 hour.

2 Crumble cake into large bowl. Stir in frosting until well blended. Refrigerate about 2 hours or until firm enough to shape.

3 Roll cake mixture into 48 (1½-inch) balls; place on cookie sheet. Freeze 1 to 2 hours or until firm. Meanwhile, coarsely crush cereal. Line cookie sheet with waxed paper.

4 In 1-quart microwavable bowl, microwave 12 oz of the candy coating uncovered on High 1 minute 30 seconds; stir. Continue microwaving and stirring in 15-second increments until melted; stir until smooth. Remove 16 of the balls from freezer. Using 2 forks, dip and roll each ball in coating. Place on waxed paper–lined cookie sheet. Immediately sprinkle with crushed cereal. Melt remaining candy coating in 12-oz batches; dip remaining balls and sprinkle with cereal. Transfer to refrigerator.

5 To serve, carefully insert 1 lollipop stick into 1 cake ball no more than halfway. Poke opposite end of stick into foam block. Store any remaining cake balls in tightly covered container in refrigerator.

1 Cake Pop: Calories 220; Total Fat 11g (Saturated Fat 5g, Trans Fat 0.5g); Cholesterol 20mg; Sodium 125mg; Total Carbohydrate 29g (Dietary Fiber 0g); Protein 2g **Carbohydrate Choices:** 2

Gusher Confetti Cake Balls

Prep Time: 1 Hour 20 Minutes • **Start to Finish:** 3 Hours • Makes 48 cake balls

- 1 box Betty Crocker SuperMoist rainbow chip cake mix
- Water, vegetable oil and eggs called for on cake mix box
- 1 cup Betty Crocker Rich & Creamy vanilla frosting (from 1-lb container)
- 1 cup multicolored candy sprinkles
- 5 pouches (0.9 oz each) Betty Crocker Fruit Gushers fruit snacks, tropical flavors (from 5.4-oz box)
- 2 bags (16 oz each) white or dark cocoa candy melts or coating wafers

1 Heat oven to 350°F (325°F for dark or nonstick pan). Make and bake cake mix as directed on box for 13 x 9-inch pan, using water, oil and eggs. Cool completely, about 1 hour.

2 Line cookie sheets with waxed paper. Crumble cake into large bowl. Add frosting and ½ cup of the sprinkles; mix well. Shape into 48 (1¼-inch) balls. Press 1 fruit snack into each ball, covering completely; place on cookie sheets. Freeze until firm; transfer to refrigerator.

3 In medium microwavable bowl, microwave 1 bag of candy melts uncovered on Medium (50%) 1 minute; stir. Continue microwaving and stirring in 15-second increments, until melted; stir until smooth. Remove several cake balls from refrigerator at a time. Dip cake balls into melted candy to cover; tap off excess. Place on cooking parchment paper. Immediately sprinkle with some of the remaining ½ cup sprinkles. Let stand until set. Repeat with remaining bag of candy melts, cake balls and sprinkles.

1 Cake Ball: Calories 213; Total Fat 11g (Saturated Fat 6g, Trans Fat 0g); Cholesterol 0mg; Sodium 90mg; Total Carbohydrate 29g (Dietary Fiber 0g); Protein 1g **Carbohydrate Choices:** 2

Sports Ball Cake Pops

Prep Time: 1 Hour 35 Minutes • **Start to Finish:** 4 Hours • Makes 28 cake pops

Cake

- 1 cup Gold Medal® all-purpose flour
- ½ teaspoon baking soda
- ½ teaspoon baking powder
- ¼ teaspoon salt
- ¾ cup granulated sugar
- ¼ cup butter, softened
- ½ cup sour cream
- 2 egg whites
- 1 teaspoon vanilla
- ¼ cup milk

Filling

- 2 cups powdered sugar
- 3 tablespoons butter, softened
- 1 tablespoon milk
- 1 teaspoon vanilla
- 8 creme-filled chocolate sandwich cookies, coarsely crushed (about 1 cup)

Coating and Decorations

- 2 bags (12 oz each) candy melts of desired color
- 28 paper lollipop sticks
- 2 blocks of white plastic craft foam
- Icing writer or food decorating pen of desired color

1 Heat oven to 350°F. Grease 8- or 9-inch round pan with shortening; lightly flour. In medium bowl, mix flour, baking soda, baking powder and salt; set aside.

2 In large bowl, beat granulated sugar and ¼ cup butter with electric mixer on medium speed about 2 minutes or until light and fluffy, scraping bowl occasionally. Beat in sour cream. Beat in egg whites, one at a time, beating well after each addition. Beat in 1 teaspoon vanilla. On low speed, alternately add flour mixture, about one-third at a time, and milk, about half at a time, beating just until blended. Pour into pan.

3 Bake 33 to 38 minutes or until top springs back when touched lightly in center. Cool 15 minutes.

4 Meanwhile, in medium bowl, mix powdered sugar and 3 tablespoons butter with electric mixer on low speed until blended. Beat in 1 tablespoon milk and 1 teaspoon vanilla. Crumble cake into medium bowl. Stir powdered sugar mixture into crumbled cake until well blended. Stir in crushed cookies. Cover; refrigerate 1 to 2 hours or until firm enough to shape. Roll cake mixture into 28 (1½-inch) balls; place on waxed paper–lined cookie sheet. Freeze 30 minutes.

5 In 2-cup microwavable measuring cup, microwave 12 oz of the candy melts as directed on package until melted. Coating must be at least 3 inches deep; add more candy melts as necessary to reach and/or maintain 3-inch depth. Remove several cake balls from freezer at a time. Dip tip of 1 lollipop stick ½ inch into melted candy and carefully insert stick into 1 cake ball no more than halfway. Dip cake ball into melted candy to cover; tap off excess. (Reheat candy in microwave or add vegetable oil if too thick to coat.) Poke opposite end of stick into foam block. With icing writer, decorate cake pops to resemble desired sports balls. Let stand until set.

1 Cake Pop: Calories 130; Total Fat 4.5g (Saturated Fat 2.5g, Trans Fat 0g); Cholesterol 10mg; Sodium 105mg; Total Carbohydrate 20g (Dietary Fiber 0g); Protein 1g **Carbohydrate Choices:** 1

Tip Crush the cookies quickly by placing them in a resealable food-storage plastic bag and crushing them with a rolling pin.

Watermelon Cake Pops

Prep Time: 1 Hour • **Start to Finish:** 3 Hours 10 Minutes • Makes 32 cake pops

1 box Betty Crocker SuperMoist white cake mix

Water, vegetable oil and egg whites called for on cake mix box

¼ teaspoon pink paste food color

¾ cup Betty Crocker Rich & Creamy vanilla frosting (from 1-lb container)

¾ cup miniature semisweet chocolate chips

32 paper lollipop sticks

1 bag (16 oz) white candy melts or coating wafers, melted

1 block of white plastic craft foam

1 bag (16 oz) green candy melts or coating wafers, melted

1 cup light green candy melts (from 16-oz bag), melted

1 Heat oven to 350°F (325°F for dark or nonstick pan). Spray 13 x 9-inch pan with cooking spray. Make and bake cake mix as directed on box for 13 x 9-inch pan, using water, oil and egg whites and adding pink paste food color. Cool completely, about 1 hour.

2 Line cookie sheet with waxed paper. Crumble cake into large bowl. Add frosting and chocolate chips; mix well. Shape into 32 oblong balls; place on cookie sheet. Freeze until firm; transfer to refrigerator.

3 Remove several cake balls from refrigerator at a time. Dip tip of 1 lollipop stick ½ inch into melted white candy and carefully insert stick into 1 cake ball no more than halfway. Dip cake ball into melted candy to cover; tap off excess. Poke opposite end of stick into foam block. Let stand until set. Dip each cake ball into melted green candy to cover; tap off excess. Return sticks to foam block. Let stand until set. With toothpick, decorate cake balls with light green candy to look like watermelons. Let stand until set.

1 Cake Pop: Calories 351; Total Fat 17g (Saturated Fat 10g, Trans Fat 0g); Cholesterol 0mg; Sodium 119mg; Total Carbohydrate 49g (Dietary Fiber 0g); Protein 1g **Carbohydrate Choices:** 3

Cookies-and-Cream Cake Pops

Prep Time: 50 Minutes • **Start to Finish:** 2 Hours 30 Minutes • Makes 84 cake pops

- 1 box Betty Crocker SuperMoist white cake mix
- Water, vegetable oil and egg whites called for on cake mix box
- 12 creme-filled chocolate sandwich cookies, crushed (1 cup)
- 1 cup Betty Crocker Whipped cream cheese frosting (from 12-oz container)
- 84 paper lollipop sticks
- 2 cups green candy melts or coating wafers, melted (from 12-oz bag)
- 2 blocks of white plastic craft foam
- 2 cups light blue candy melts or coating wafers, melted (from 12-oz bag)
- 2 cups yellow candy melts or coating wafers, melted (from 12-oz bag)
- ¾ cup white vanilla baking chips
- 2 tablespoons coarse white sparkling sugar

1 Make and bake cake mix as directed on box for 13 x 9-inch pan, using water, oil and egg whites. Cool completely, about 1 hour. Line 2 cookie sheets with waxed paper. Crumble cake into large bowl. Add crushed cookies and frosting; mix well. Shape into 84 (1-inch) balls; place on cookie sheets. Freeze about 15 minutes or until firm; transfer to refrigerator.

2 Remove 28 cake balls from refrigerator. Dip tip of 1 lollipop stick ½ inch into melted green candy and carefully insert stick into 1 cake ball no more than halfway. Dip cake ball into melted candy to cover; tap off excess. Poke opposite end of stick into foam block. Repeat with remaining cake balls, coating 28 with blue candy and 28 with yellow candy. In small resealable freezer plastic bag, place white chips; seal bag. Microwave on High about 1 minute or until softened. Gently squeeze bag until chocolate is smooth; cut off tiny corner of bag. Squeeze bag to drizzle melted chips over cake pops. Immediately sprinkle with sparkling sugar.

1 Cake Pop: Calories 110; Total Fat 6g (Saturated Fat 4g, Trans Fat 0g); Cholesterol 0mg; Sodium 79mg; Total Carbohydrate 18g (Dietary Fiber 0g); Protein 0g **Carbohydrate Choices:** 1

Scaredy Cat Cake Pops

Prep Time: 1 Hour • **Start to Finish:** 3 Hours 30 Minutes • Makes 28 cake pops

1 box Betty Crocker SuperMoist vanilla cake mix

Water, vegetable oil and eggs called for on cake mix box

¾ cup Betty Crocker Rich & Creamy vanilla frosting (from 1-lb container)

⅓ cup orange candy sprinkles

Black food decorating pen

56 sliced almonds (⅛ cup)

14 strands rice stick noodles

2 bags (10 oz each) black candy melts or coating wafers

½ teaspoon black candy coating

2 tablespoons canola oil

28 paper lollipop sticks

1 block of white plastic craft foam

56 pieces candy corn (⅔ cup)

1 Heat oven to 350°F. Make and bake cake mix as directed on box for 13 x 9-inch pan, using water, oil and eggs. Cool completely, about 1 hour.

2 Line cookie sheet with waxed paper. Crumble cake into large bowl. Add frosting and candy sprinkles; mix well. Shape into 1½-inch balls. Place on cookie sheet. Freeze until firm; transfer to refrigerator.

3 Using black decorating pen, draw eye pupils on almonds. Let stand until set. Break rice stick noodles into 1½-inch pieces; set aside.

4 In medium microwavable bowl, microwave candy melts uncovered on Medium (50%) 1 minute, then in 15-second increments, until melted; stir until smooth. Stir in ½ teaspoon candy coating. Stir in oil. Remove several cake balls from refrigerator at a time. Dip tip of 1 lollipop stick about ½ inch into melted candy and carefully insert stick into 1 cake ball no more than halfway. Dip cake ball into melted candy to cover; tap off excess. (Reheat candy in microwave or add vegetable oil if too thick to coat.) Poke opposite end of stick into foam block.

5 Immediately attach 2 pieces candy corn to top of each cake pop for ears; attach almonds for eyes and insert rice stick noodles for whiskers. Let stand until set. Repeat with remaining cake balls.

1 Cake Pop: Calories 267; Total Fat 14g (Saturated Fat 6g, Trans Fat 0g); Cholesterol 0mg; Sodium 128mg; Total Carbohydrate 36g (Dietary Fiber 0g); Protein 2g **Carbohydrate Choices:** 2½

Tip For a cute display, insert the foam block into a clay pot and cover it with a mix of orange candy-coated chocolate candies and sprinkles.

Witchy Cake Balls

Prep Time: 1 Hour • **Start to Finish:** 1 Hour 40 Minutes • Makes 12 cake balls

1 box Betty Crocker SuperMoist chocolate fudge cake mix

Water, vegetable oil and eggs called for on cake mix box

1 container (1 lb) Betty Crocker Rich & Creamy chocolate frosting

8 oz dark cocoa candy melts or coating wafers

12 sugar-style ice cream cones with pointed ends

Assorted Halloween candy sprinkles or nonpareils

12 thin chocolate wafer cookies

1 bag (16 oz) green or dark green candy melts or coating wafers

1 tube (4.25 oz) green decorating icing

4 pull-and-peel black or red licorice twists, separated, cut into 2½-inch pieces

24 candy-coated chocolate candies

12 pieces candy corn

1 Heat oven to 350°F. Grease bottom only of 13 x 9-inch pan with shortening or cooking spray. Make and bake cake mix as directed on box for 13 x 9-inch pan, using water, oil and eggs. Cool 10 minutes; remove cake from pan to cooling rack. Cool 15 minutes.

2 Line cookie sheet with waxed paper. Crumble cake into large bowl. Add chocolate frosting; mix well with back of spoon. Use ice cream scoop to scoop cake mixture into 12 (2½-inch) balls onto cookie sheet. Freeze about 15 minutes or until firm; transfer to refrigerator.

3 In medium microwavable bowl, microwave dark cocoa candy melts uncovered on Medium (50%) 1 minute, then in 15-second increments, until melted; stir until smooth. Using small food-safe brush, brush melted chocolate coating over each ice cream cone to coat completely. Decorate as desired with sprinkles before coating hardens. Dip open end of each ice cream cone into remaining melted chocolate coating; place dipped end of each cone onto a chocolate wafer cookie, pressing lightly, to form hat and brim. Let stand until set.

4 In medium microwavable bowl, microwave green candy melts uncovered on Medium (50%) 1 minute, then in 15-second increments, until melted; stir until smooth. Remove several cake balls from refrigerator at a time. Place 1 cake ball on a fork; dip cake ball into melted green coating to cover and tap off excess. Place coated ball on cookie sheet; top with 1 chocolate-coated cone hat, pressing gently. Repeat with remaining cake balls and cone hats. Let stand until set.

5 Pipe decorating icing onto bottom edge of each chocolate wafer cookie; attach licorice pieces with icing to form hair (about 12 pieces licorice per cake ball). Use icing to attach 2 chocolate candies in front of each ball for eyes and 1 piece candy corn for nose.

1 Cake Ball: Calories 792; Total Fat 35g (Saturated Fat 17g, Trans Fat 0g); Cholesterol 0mg; Sodium 546mg; Total Carbohydrate 115g (Dietary Fiber 3g); Protein 6g **Carbohydrate Choices:** 7½

Tip For a quick treat, just make and enjoy the candy-coated cake ball portion of this recipe.

Special Occasions

Strawberries-and-Cream Cake Pops

Prep Time: 40 Minutes • **Start to Finish:** 2 Hours 10 Minutes • Makes 36 cake pops

1 box Betty Crocker SuperMoist white cake mix

Water, vegetable oil and egg whites called for on cake mix box

½ cup powdered sugar

2 oz cream cheese, softened

¼ cup butter, softened

¼ cup strawberry jam

1 cup dried strawberries, chopped

1 cup red candy melts (from 14-oz bag), melted

2 bags (14 oz each) pink candy melts or coating wafers, melted

36 paper lollipop sticks

1 block of white plastic craft foam

½ cup pink colored sugar

1 Heat oven to 350°F (325°F for dark or nonstick pan). Spray 13 x 9-inch pan with cooking spray. Make and bake cake mix as directed on box for 13 x 9-inch pan, using water, oil and egg whites. Cool completely, about 1 hour.

2 Line cookie sheet with waxed paper. In large bowl, beat powdered sugar, cream cheese, butter and jam with electric mixer on medium speed until blended. Crumble cake into cream cheese mixture; mix well. Stir in dried strawberries. Shape into 36 (2-inch) balls; place on cookie sheet. Freeze until firm; transfer to refrigerator.

3 Spoon about 2 tablespoons melted red candy into pink candy; swirl gently. Remove several cake balls from refrigerator at a time. Dip tip of 1 lollipop stick about ½ inch into melted candy and carefully insert stick into 1 cake ball no more than halfway. Dip each cake ball into swirled candy to cover; tap off excess. (Reheat candy in microwave or add vegetable oil if too thick to coat; spoon more red candy into pink candy as needed.) Poke opposite end of stick into foam block. Sprinkle with pink sugar. Let stand until set.

1 Cake Pop: Calories 278; Total Fat 13g (Saturated Fat 7g, Trans Fat 0g); Cholesterol 0mg; Sodium 118mg; Total Carbohydrate 40g (Dietary Fiber 0g); Protein 1g **Carbohydrate Choices:** 2½

Lemon Meringue Cake Pops

Prep Time: 50 Minutes • **Start to Finish:** 2 Minutes 55 Minutes • Makes 48 cake pops

3 cups Gold Medal all-purpose flour

4½ teaspoons baking powder

½ teaspoon salt

1 cup milk

2 teaspoons vanilla

1 teaspoon grated lemon peel

5 egg whites

1¾ cups granulated sugar

1 cup butter or margarine, softened

1 jar (10 oz) lemon curd (about 1 cup)

1 box (7.2 oz) Betty Crocker HomeStyle fluffy white frosting mix

½ cup boiling water

48 paper lollipop sticks

2 blocks of white plastic craft foam

¼ cup coarse yellow sparkling sugar

1 Heat oven to 350°F. Grease bottom and sides of 13 x 9-inch pan with shortening; lightly flour.

2 In medium bowl, mix flour, baking powder and salt; set aside. In small bowl, mix milk, vanilla, lemon peel and egg whites; set aside. In large bowl, beat granulated sugar and butter with electric mixer on medium speed until light and fluffy. On low speed, alternately add flour mixture and milk mixture, beating just until blended after each addition. Pour into pan.

3 Bake 30 to 35 minutes or until toothpick inserted in center comes out clean. Cool completely, about 1 hour.

4 Line cookie sheet with waxed paper. Crumble cake into large bowl. Add lemon curd; mix well with spoon. Roll cake mixture into 48 (1-inch) balls; place on cookie sheet. Freeze about 30 minutes or until firm; keep frozen.

5 In medium deep bowl, beat frosting mix and boiling water with electric mixer on low speed 30 seconds, scraping bowl constantly. Beat on high speed 5 to 7 minutes, scraping bowl occasionally, until stiff glossy peaks form.

6 Remove several cake balls from freezer at a time. Carefully insert 1 lollipop stick into 1 cake ball no more than halfway. Dip cake ball into frosting, swirling to coat. Poke opposite end of stick into foam block. Sprinkle cake pop with sparkling sugar.

1 Cake Pop: Calories 133; Total Fat 5g (Saturated Fat 3g, Trans Fat 0g); Cholesterol 0mg; Sodium 121mg; Total Carbohydrate 22g (Dietary Fiber 0g); Protein 1g **Carbohydrate Choices:** 1½

Tip A mock meringue coats these cake balls infused with tangy lemon curd. Store them loosely covered in the refrigerator.

Tequila Sunrise Cake Pops

Prep Time: 1 Hour 5 Minutes • **Start to Finish:** 3 Hours 10 Minutes • Makes 18 cake pops

Cake

1 cup Gold Medal all-purpose flour
⅓ cup granulated sugar
1 tablespoon grated orange peel
1 teaspoon baking powder
¼ teaspoon baking soda
¼ teaspoon salt
¼ cup orange juice
¼ cup vegetable oil
2 tablespoons orange-flavored liqueur
1 tablespoon grenadine syrup
2 eggs

Filling

¼ cup butter, softened
1½ cups powdered sugar
3 tablespoons tequila

Coating

1 bag (12 oz) yellow candy melts or coating wafers
28 paper lollipop sticks
2 blocks of white plastic craft foam
1 bag (12 oz) orange candy melts or coating wafers
Red colored sugar

1 Heat oven to 350°F. Spray bottom only of 8 x 4-inch loaf pan with cooking spray. In large bowl, combine all cake ingredients. Beat with electric mixer on low speed until mixed. Beat on medium speed 2 minutes. Pour into pan.

2 Bake 30 to 35 minutes or until toothpick inserted in center comes out clean. Cool 10 minutes; remove from pan to cooling rack. Cool completely, about 50 minutes. Trim browned edges from sides and bottom of cake.

3 Into food processor with metal blade, crumble half of cake. Cover; process with on-and-off pulses until cake is fine crumbs. Place in large bowl; repeat with remaining cake.

4 In small bowl, combine all filling ingredients; beat with electric mixer on low speed until mixed. Beat on medium speed until creamy. Add filling to cake crumbs and mix until all crumbs are moistened and mixture holds together. Roll into 18 (1½-inch) balls; place on waxed paper–lined cookie sheet. Freeze 30 minutes.

5 In 2-cup microwavable measuring cup, microwave yellow candy melts as directed on package until melted. Remove several cake balls from freezer at a time. Dip tip of 1 lollipop stick about ½ inch into melted coating and carefully insert stick into 1 cake ball no more than halfway. Dip cake ball into melted candy to cover; tap off excess. (Reheat candy in microwave or add vegetable oil if too thick to coat.) Poke opposite end of stick into foam block. Let stand until set.

6 In another 2-cup microwavable measuring cup, microwave orange candy melts as directed on package until melted. Dip bottom half of each yellow-coated cake pop into orange melted candy. Dip tops into red colored sugar. Poke opposite end of stick back into foam block. Let stand until set.

1 Cake Pop: Calories 350; Total Fat 17g (Saturated Fat 12g, Trans Fat 0g); Cholesterol 30mg; Sodium 150mg; Total Carbohydrate 46g (Dietary Fiber 0g); Protein 1g **Carbohydrate Choices:** 3

Tip You can find the candy melts at your local craft store in the candy-making and cake decorating section.

Chocolate-Covered Cherry Cake Pops

Prep Time: 50 Minutes • **Start to Finish:** 2 Hours 45 Minutes • Makes 28 cake pops

- 1 box Betty Crocker SuperMoist vanilla cake mix
- Water, vegetable oil and eggs called for on cake mix box
- ¾ cup Betty Crocker Rich & Creamy vanilla frosting (from 1-lb container)
- 28 maraschino cherries, stems removed
- 1 package (16 oz) chocolate-flavored candy coating, chopped
- 28 paper lollipop sticks
- 1 block of white plastic craft foam
- 2 tablespoons red sugar crystals

1 Heat oven to 350°F (325°F for dark or nonstick pan). Make and bake cake mix as directed on box for 13 x 9-inch pan, using water, oil and eggs. Cool completely, about 1 hour.

2 Line cookie sheet with waxed paper. Crumble cake into large bowl. Add frosting; mix well. Shape into 28 (1½-inch) balls, placing cherry in center of each and covering cherry completely. Place on cookie sheet. Freeze until firm; transfer to refrigerator.

3 In medium microwavable bowl, microwave candy coating on Medium (50%) 1 minute, then in 15-second increments, until melted; stir until smooth. Remove several cake balls from refrigerator at a time. Dip tip of 1 lollipop stick about ½ inch into melted candy and carefully insert stick into 1 cake ball no more than halfway. Dip cake ball into melted candy to cover; tap off excess. Poke opposite end of stick into foam block. Sprinkle cake pop with sugar crystals. Let stand until set.

1 Cake Pop: Calories 224; Total Fat 11g (Saturated Fat 5g, Trans Fat 0g); Cholesterol 0mg; Sodium 138mg; Total Carbohydrate 31g (Dietary Fiber 0g); Protein 2g **Carbohydrate Choices:** 2

Boston Cream Cake Pops

Prep Time: 50 Minutes • **Start to Finish:** 3 Hours 35 Minutes • Makes 24 cake pops

- 1 box Betty Crocker SuperMoist yellow cake mix
- Water, vegetable oil and eggs called for on cake mix box
- 3 tablespoons sugar
- 1 tablespoon cornstarch
- Dash salt
- 1 cup milk
- 2 egg yolks, beaten
- 1 tablespoon butter or margarine
- ½ teaspoon vanilla or vanilla bean paste
- 24 paper lollipop sticks
- 1 package (16 oz) chocolate-flavored candy coating, chopped, melted
- 1 block of white plastic craft foam
- ½ cup white vanilla baking chips
- ½ teaspoon shortening

1 Heat oven to 350°F (325°F for dark or nonstick pan). Spray bottom only of 13 x 9-inch pan with cooking spray. Make and bake cake mix as directed on box for 13 x 9-inch pan, using water, oil and eggs. Cool completely, about 1 hour.

2 Meanwhile, in 2-quart saucepan, mix sugar, cornstarch and salt. Add milk and egg yolks. Cook and stir over medium heat until mixture boils. Boil 1 minute. Stir in butter and vanilla. Remove from heat. Cover surface of pudding with plastic wrap; cool.

3 Line cookie sheet with waxed paper. Crumble cake into large bowl. Add pudding; mix well with fingers until mixture is well combined. Shape into 24 (1½-inch) balls; place on cookie sheet. Freeze until firm; transfer to refrigerator.

4 Remove several cake balls from refrigerator at a time. Dip tip of 1 lollipop stick about ½ inch into melted candy and carefully insert stick into 1 cake ball no more than halfway. Dip each cake ball into melted candy to cover; tap off excess. Poke opposite end of stick into foam block. Let stand until set. In small microwavable bowl, melt baking chips with shortening; drizzle over pops. Let stand until set.

1 Cake Pop: Calories 262; Total Fat 13g (Saturated Fat 7g, Trans Fat 0g); Cholesterol 0mg; Sodium 178mg; Total Carbohydrate 34g (Dietary Fiber 0g); Protein 3g **Carbohydrate Choices:** 2½

Raspberry-Chocolate Cake Pops

Prep Time: 1 Hour 30 Minutes • **Start to Finish:** 4 Hours • Makes 28 cake pops

Cake

1¼ cups Gold Medal all-purpose flour
1¾ teaspoons baking powder
½ teaspoon salt
¼ cup butter, softened
¾ cup granulated sugar
3 egg whites
½ teaspoon vanilla
½ cup milk

Truffles

8 oz semisweet baking chocolate, finely chopped
4 teaspoons raspberry-flavored vodka
¼ cup whipping cream
2 tablespoons butter

Filling

⅓ cup butter, softened
2½ cups powdered sugar
2 tablespoons raspberry-flavored vodka

Coating

1 bag (12 oz) dark chocolate candy melts or coating wafers
1 bag (12 oz) light cocoa candy melts or coating wafers
28 paper lollipop sticks (6 inch)

1 Heat oven to 350°F. Grease 8- or 9-inch round pan with shortening; lightly flour. In small bowl, mix flour, baking powder and salt. In medium bowl, beat ¼ cup butter with electric mixer on medium speed 30 seconds. Beat in granulated sugar, ¼ cup at a time, beating well after each addition. Beat 2 minutes longer, scraping bowl occasionally. Add egg whites, one at a time, beating well after each addition. Beat in vanilla. On low speed, alternately add flour mixture, about one-third at a time, and milk, about one-half at a time, beating just until blended. Spread in pan.

2 Bake 35 to 40 minutes or until toothpick inserted in center comes out clean. Cool 20 minutes. Crumble cake into medium bowl; set aside.

3 Line cookie sheet with waxed paper. In small bowl, place chopped chocolate and 4 teaspoons raspberry vodka. In small microwavable bowl, microwave whipping cream and 2 tablespoons butter on High 1 minute or until boiling. Stir until butter is melted. Pour over chocolate mixture; stir until chocolate is melted and smooth. If necessary, microwave on High an additional 10 to 15 seconds until mixture can be stirred smooth. Pour into 8-inch square (2-quart) glass baking dish; cover and refrigerate 1 hour. When firm, use melon baller to create 28 round truffle centers. Place on cookie sheet; refrigerate until needed.

4 In medium bowl, beat ⅓ cup butter with electric mixer on medium speed until smooth. Gradually beat in powdered sugar and 2 tablespoons raspberry vodka on low speed until filling is smooth. Stir into crumbled cake until blended. Cover; refrigerate 1 to 2 hours or until firm enough to shape.

5 Line cookie sheet with waxed paper. Shape cake mixture into 28 (1½-inch) balls. On sheet of waxed paper, flatten each ball into 3-inch round. Place truffle in center of each round. Quickly shape round up and around truffle (overhandling can cause truffle to melt), pinching round together to seal and sealing any cracks. Place on cookie sheet. Freeze 30 minutes.

6 In 2-cup microwavable measuring cup, microwave dark chocolate candy melts as directed on package until melted. Remove several cake balls from freezer at a time. Dip tip of each of 14 lollipop sticks about ½ inch into melted dark chocolate and carefully insert into each of 14 cake balls no more than halfway. Dip cake ball into melted candy to cover; tap off excess. (Reheat candy in microwave or add vegetable oil if too thick to coat.) Place each cake ball in mini cupcake liner. Reserve remaining coating. Repeat with light cocoa candy melts and remaining 14 cake balls. Let stand until set. Use remaining melted candy (remelt, if necessary) to drizzle dark chocolate over light cocoa cake pops and light cocoa over dark chocolate cake pops. Let stand 15 minutes or until set.

1 Cake Pop: Calories 320; Total Fat 17g (Saturated Fat 12g, Trans Fat 0g); Cholesterol 15mg; Sodium 150mg; Total Carbohydrate 40g (Dietary Fiber 1g); Protein 2g **Carbohydrate Choices:** 2½

Tip Raspberry vodka adds a nice berry flavor without turning the cake and filling purple-grey, like traditional black raspberry liqueur.

Cappuccino Cake Pops

Prep Time: 1 Hour 40 Minutes • **Start to Finish:** 3 Hours 45 Minutes • Makes 50 cake pops

½ cup hot water

6 tablespoons instant espresso coffee powder or granules

1 cup plus 2 tablespoons Gold Medal all-purpose flour

½ teaspoon baking soda

¼ teaspoon salt

⅔ cup sugar

¼ cup butter or margarine, softened

2 eggs

2 tablespoons coffee-flavored liqueur

¼ cup buttermilk

2 containers (12 oz each) Betty Crocker Whipped milk chocolate frosting

50 paper lollipop sticks

2 blocks of white plastic craft foam

½ cup Betty Crocker Whipped fluffy white frosting (from 12-oz container)

50 chocolate-covered coffee beans (about 1 cup)

2 tablespoons unsweetened baking cocoa

1 Heat oven to 350°F. Grease bottom and sides of 8-inch square pan with shortening; lightly flour.

2 In small bowl, stir hot water and coffee powder until coffee is dissolved; set aside. In medium bowl, mix flour, baking soda and salt; set aside.

3 In large bowl, beat sugar and butter with electric mixer on medium speed until light and fluffy. Beat in eggs, one at a time, just until blended. Beat in liqueur and coffee mixture. On low speed, alternately add flour mixture and buttermilk, beating just until blended after each addition. Pour into pan.

4 Bake 28 to 30 minutes or until toothpick inserted in center comes out clean. Cool 10 minutes; remove from pan to cooling rack. Cool completely, about 45 minutes.

5 Line cookie sheet with waxed paper. Crumble cake into large bowl. Add ½ cup of the chocolate frosting; mix well with spoon. Roll into 50 (1-inch) balls; place on cookie sheet. Freeze about 30 minutes or until firm; transfer to refrigerator.

6 In medium microwavable bowl, microwave remaining chocolate frosting uncovered on Medium (50%) 30 seconds or until melted; stir until smooth. Remove several cake balls from refrigerator at a time. Dip tip of 1 lollipop stick about ½ inch into melted frosting and carefully insert stick into 1 cake ball no more than halfway. Dip cake ball into melted frosting to cover; tap off excess. Poke opposite end of stick into foam block. Let stand until set.

7 In small microwavable bowl, microwave white frosting uncovered on Medium (50%) 10 to 20 seconds or until melted; stir until smooth. Spoon ½ teaspoon frosting on top of each cake pop, letting it drip down side slightly. Immediately top with coffee bean. Poke opposite end of stick back into foam block. Let stand until set. Sprinkle lightly with cocoa. Store loosely covered in refrigerator.

1 Cake Pop: Calories 109; Total Fat 5g (Saturated Fat 2g, Trans Fat 0g); Cholesterol 0mg; Sodium 78mg; Total Carbohydrate 15g (Dietary Fiber 0g); Protein 1g **Carbohydrate Choices:** 1

Maple-Walnut Cake Pops

Prep Time: 1 Hour • **Start to Finish:** 3 Hours 35 Minutes • Makes 48 cake pops

1 box Betty Crocker SuperMoist vanilla cake mix

Water, vegetable oil and eggs called for on cake mix box

10 slices packaged precooked bacon (from 2.1-oz package), crisply cooked, crumbled

2 cups chopped walnuts

3½ teaspoons maple flavor

⅔ cup Betty Crocker Rich & Creamy cream cheese frosting (from 1-lb container)

1 tablespoon real maple syrup

¾ cup sugar

2 containers (1 lb each) Betty Crocker Rich & Creamy cream cheese frosting

48 paper lollipop sticks

1 Heat oven to 350°F (325°F for dark or nonstick pan). Spray 13 x 9-inch pan with cooking spray. Make cake mix as directed on box for 13 x 9-inch pan, using water, oil and eggs; stir in bacon, 1¼ cups of the walnuts and 2½ teaspoons of the maple flavor. Pour into pan. Bake as directed for 13 x 9-inch pan. Cool completely, about 1 hour.

2 Line cookie sheet with waxed paper. Crumble cake into large bowl. Add ⅔ cup frosting and the syrup; mix well. Shape into 48 (1¼-inch) balls. Place on cookie sheet. Freeze until firm; transfer to refrigerator.

3 In 12-inch skillet, cook sugar over medium heat, stirring constantly, until melted and golden. Remove from heat; place remaining ¾ cup walnuts in sugar mixture, turning to coat. With fork, remove walnuts to waxed paper; cool completely. Into large microwavable bowl, spoon 2 containers frosting. Microwave on Medium (50%) 30 seconds or until melted; stir until smooth. Stir in remaining 1 teaspoon maple flavor. Remove several cake balls from refrigerator at a time. Dip tip of 1 lollipop stick about ½ inch into melted frosting and carefully insert into 1 cake ball no more than halfway. Dip cake ball into melted frosting to cover; tap off excess. Top with sugared nuts. Poke opposite end of stick back into foam block.

1 Cake Pop: Calories 210; Total Fat 11g (Saturated Fat 2g, Trans Fat 0g); Cholesterol 0mg; Sodium 145mg; Total Carbohydrate 25g (Dietary Fiber 0g); Protein 2g **Carbohydrate Choices:** 1½

Bourbon-Spiked Brownie Truffle Balls

Prep Time: 35 Minutes • **Start to Finish:** 2 Hours 5 Minutes • Makes 60 truffle balls

Truffles

1 box (1 lb 2.3 oz) Betty Crocker fudge brownie mix
⅔ cup butter, melted
3 eggs
½ cup miniature semisweet chocolate chips
½ cup bourbon
½ teaspoon ground ginger
2 cups crushed gingersnap cookies (about 40 cookies)

Garnish, if desired

½ cup semisweet chocolate chips, melted
½ cup white vanilla baking chips, melted
½ cup finely chopped crystallized ginger

1 Heat oven to 350°F. Spray bottom only of 13 x 9-inch pan with cooking spray.

2 In medium bowl, stir brownie mix, melted butter, eggs, miniature chocolate chips, ¼ cup of the bourbon, the ground ginger and crushed cookies until well blended. Spread in pan.

3 Bake 24 to 26 minutes or until toothpick inserted 1 inch from side of pan comes out almost clean. Cool completely, about 1 hour.

4 In medium bowl, crumble cooled brownies into chunks; stir in remaining ¼ cup bourbon. Shape into 60 (1-inch) balls. Drizzle or coat with melted chocolate and white chips; sprinkle with crystallized ginger.

1 Truffle Ball: Calories 80; Total Fat 3.5g (Saturated Fat 1.5g, Trans Fat 0g); Cholesterol 15mg; Sodium 75mg; Total Carbohydrate 12g (Dietary Fiber 0g); Protein 0g **Carbohydrate Choices:** 1

Tip Brownies can be made ahead and stored in a tightly covered container at room temperature up to 2 days or in the freezer up to 1 month. Just for fun, serve the truffle balls in shot glasses or small cupcake liners.

Cake Ball Ornaments

Prep Time: 1 Hour 15 Minutes • **Start to Finish:** 3 Hours • Makes 45 cake balls

- 1 box Betty Crocker SuperMoist German chocolate cake mix
- 1 cup buttermilk
- ½ cup vegetable oil
- 3 eggs
- 2 tablespoons unsweetened baking cocoa
- 1 bottle (1 oz) red food color
- 1 cup Betty Crocker Rich & Creamy cream cheese frosting (from 1-lb container)
- 2 cups green candy melts or coating wafers, melted
- 2 cups red candy melts or coating wafers, melted
- 1 cup white candy melts or coating wafers, melted
- 90 pieces Frosted Cheerios® cereal (about ⅓ cup)

1 Heat oven to 350°F (325°F for dark or nonstick pan). Spray 13 x 9-inch pan with cooking spray. In large bowl, beat cake mix, buttermilk, oil, eggs, cocoa and food color with electric mixer on medium speed 2 minutes. Pour into pan. Bake 25 to 30 minutes or until toothpick inserted in center comes out clean. Cool completely, about 1 hour.

2 Line cookie sheet with waxed paper. Crumble cake into large bowl. Add frosting; mix well. Shape into 45 (1¼-inch) balls. Place on cookie sheet. Freeze about 15 minutes or until firm; transfer to refrigerator.

3 Remove several cake balls from refrigerator at a time. Dip half of balls in melted green candy and other half in melted red candy; tap off excess. Return to cookie sheet; let stand until set.

4 Spoon melted white candy into resealable food-storage plastic bag; cut off tiny corner of bag. Pipe designs on cake balls; let stand until set. Gently press 1 cereal piece on top of each cake ball, attaching with white candy. Pipe dot of candy on cereal piece; attach another cereal piece upright in center for ornament hook.

1 Cake Ball: Calories 240; Total Fat 12g (Saturated Fat 6g, Trans Fat 0g); Cholesterol 0mg; Sodium 110mg; Total Carbohydrate 32g (Dietary Fiber 0g); Protein 1g **Carbohydrate Choices:** 2

Special Occasions

Holiday Cake Bon Bons

Prep Time: 35 Minutes • **Start to Finish:** 3 Hours • Makes 37 servings (2 bon bons each)

1 box Betty Crocker SuperMoist cake mix (any flavor)

Water, vegetable oil and eggs called for on cake mix box

1 container Betty Crocker Rich & Creamy frosting (any flavor)

36 oz (from two 24-oz packages) vanilla- or chocolate-flavored candy coating (almond bark)

1 Heat oven to 350°F (325°F for dark or nonstick pan). Make and bake cake as directed on box for 13 x 9-inch pan. Cool 15 minutes.

2 Crumble cake into large bowl. Add frosting; mix well. Refrigerate 1 to 2 hours or until firm enough to shape.

3 Drop cake mixture by teaspoonfuls onto cookie sheet. Shape into 74 balls. (If mixture is too sticky, refrigerate until firm enough to shape.) Freeze 30 minutes.

4 Line another cookie sheet with foil. In 1-quart microwavable bowl, microwave 12 oz of the candy coating uncovered on High 1 minute 30 seconds; stir. Continue microwaving and stirring in 15-second increments until melted; stir until smooth. Remove one-third of the balls from the freezer. Using 2 forks, dip and roll each ball in coating. Place on foil-covered cookie sheet. Decorate as desired. Refrigerate cake balls about 10 minutes or until coating is set. Melt remaining candy coating in 12-oz batches; dip remaining balls. Serve at room temperature. Store in tightly covered container.

1 Serving (2 Bon Bons): Calories 280; Total Fat 14g (Saturated Fat 7g, Trans Fat 0.5g); Cholesterol 25mg; Sodium 140mg; Total Carbohydrate 34g (Dietary Fiber 0g); Protein 2g **Carbohydrate Choices:** 2

Irish Cream Balls:
Make and bake cake as directed on box. Blend ¼ cup Irish cream liqueur with baked cake crumbs and frosting. Dip in melted chocolate. Sprinkle with white nonpareils. Serve in martini glass with Irish cream on the bottom.

Peppermint Red Velvet Balls:
Make and bake German chocolate cake mix as directed on box, using 1 cup water, ½ cup oil, 3 eggs, 1-oz bottle red food color and 2 tablespoons unsweetened baking cocoa. Mix 2 tablespoons peppermint schnapps with baked cake crumbs and frosting. Dip into melted chocolate. Sprinkle with crushed peppermint candies.

Metric Conversion Guide

Volume

U.S. Units	Canadian Metric	Australian Metric
¼ teaspoon	1 mL	1 ml
½ teaspoon	2 mL	2 ml
1 teaspoon	5 mL	5 ml
1 tablespoon	15 mL	20 ml
¼ cup	50 mL	60 ml
⅓ cup	75 mL	80 ml
½ cup	125 mL	125 ml
⅔ cup	150 mL	170 ml
¾ cup	175 mL	190 ml
1 cup	250 mL	250 ml
1 quart	1 liter	1 liter
1½ quarts	1.5 liters	1.5 liters
2 quarts	2 liters	2 liters
2½ quarts	2.5 liters	2.5 liters
3 quarts	3 liters	3 liters
4 quarts	4 liters	4 liters

Weight

U.S. Units	Canadian Metric	Australian Metric
1 ounce	30 grams	30 grams
2 ounces	55 grams	60 grams
3 ounces	85 grams	90 grams
4 ounces (¼ pound)	115 grams	125 grams
8 ounces (½ pound)	225 grams	225 grams
16 ounces (1 pound)	455 grams	500 grams
1 pound	455 grams	0.5 kilogram

Note: The recipes in this cookbook have not been developed or tested using metric measures. When converting recipes to metric, some variations in quality may be noted.

Measurements

Inches	Centimeters
1	2.5
2	5.0
3	7.5
4	10.0
5	12.5
6	15.0
7	17.5
8	20.5
9	23.0
10	25.5
11	28.0
12	30.5
13	33.0

Temperatures

Fahrenheit	Celsius
32°	0°
212°	100°
250°	120°
275°	140°
300°	150°
325°	160°
350°	180°
375°	190°
400°	200°
425°	220°
450°	230°
475°	240°
500°	260°

Recipe Testing and Calculating Nutrition Information

Recipe Testing:

- Large eggs and 2% milk were used unless otherwise indicated.
- Fat-free, low-fat, low-sodium or lite products were not used unless indicated.
- No nonstick cookware and bakeware were used unless otherwise indicated. No dark-colored, black or insulated bakeware was used.
- When a pan is specified, a metal pan was used; a baking dish or pie plate means ovenproof glass was used.
- An electric hand mixer was used for mixing only when mixer speeds are specified.

Calculating Nutrition:

- The first ingredient was used wherever a choice is given, such as ⅓ cup sour cream or plain yogurt.
- The first amount was used wherever a range is given, such as 3- to 3½-pound whole chicken.
- The first serving number was used wherever a range is given, such as 4 to 6 servings.
- "If desired" ingredients were not included.
- Only the amount of a marinade or frying oil that is absorbed was included.

America's most trusted cookbook is better than ever!

- 1,100 all-new photos, including hundreds of step-by-step images
- More than 1,500 recipes, with hundreds of inspiring variations and creative "mini" recipes for easy cooking ideas
- Brand-new features
- Gorgeous new design

Get the best edition of the *Betty Crocker Cookbook* today!

www.ingramcontent.com/pod-product-compliance
Lightning Source LLC
Chambersburg PA
CBHW071417290426
44108CB00014B/1868